Burntisland

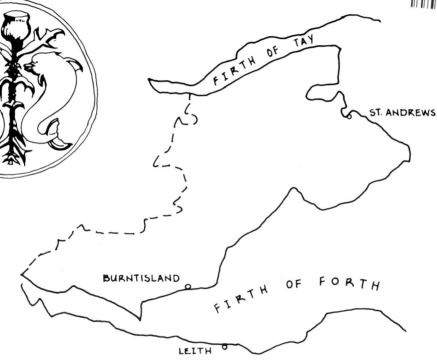

The Kingdom of Fife

FIRST EDITION
Printed May 1992

"The town is well seated, pretty strong, but marvellously capable of further improvement. The harbour at high tide is near a fathom deeper than at Leith."

Oliver Cromwell writing after the capture of Burntisland.
29th July, 1651.

John MacMillan Pearson
© Copyright 1992
ISBN 0 9519134 2 5

Printed by :-
Edmonds Advertising Ltd.
23, Mitchell Street,
Edinburgh. EH6 7BD.

Burntisland

(Twinned with Flekkefjord, Norway)

GUILD PANEL SHOWING 17th CENTURY BRIG

by John M Pearson

Burntisland's Coat of Arms

Hemmed in to the north by the Binn, a 200m high hill, Burntisland has gained a precious foothold on the shores of the Firth of Forth, and down through the centuries its prosperity has depended on this vital link with the sea.

The strategic importance of this area has been recognised since the days of Roman invasion, and the advantages of good harbour facilities surely influenced the Roman Commander Agricola, when he reputedly set up camp on nearby Dunearn Hill. In the early 12th century Burntisland Castle was built and the church at Kirkton was founded at the foot of the Binn. The first permanent settlement in the area formed around the church and was known as Wester Kingorne, which was controlled by the Abbots of Dunfermline until the 16th century. It was then, in 1541, that King James V granted Burntisland its charter as a Royal Burgh, with the main intention of developing the harbour facilities into a naval port. This proved to be a boon to Burntisland and the resultant trade encouraged the development of the town.

Due to its ever increasing importance Burntisland became involved in the historical affairs of the nation. Royalty often visited the town while en route from Edinburgh to Falkland Palace; famous people such as Vice Admiral Fairfax, his learned daughter Mary Somerville, and minister Dr Thomas Chalmers all lived here.

An increasing population in the late 16th century created a demand for a new Parish Church which was built overlooking the harbour. It still stands today and is the oldest post reformation Church in Scotland still in use. In 1601 King James VI ordered the General Assembly to meet in this Church and it was then proposed that there be a new translation of the Bible. This was known as the Authorised Version which was published in 1611.

Between 1651 and 1660 Cromwell's forces occupied Burntisland and the iron grip of the invading forces strangled the town's trade and prosperity. Yet, Burntisland recovered and in spite of similar slumps in fortune up to the present day has always bounced back to make the most of any profitable opportunity. Indeed Burntisland's importance as a naval port meant that in periods of war it was subjected to military rule and attack much to the detriment of the town. Between the 17th and 20th century various events such as the increased herring catches, the coming of the railway, the coal industry, shipbuilding and the establishment of British Alcan Aluminium Ltd. have all contributed to lifting the town out of the doldrums.

Today, Burntisland still retains an industrial presence, ferry services to Granton have been revived and the renowned Links still provides an area for entertainment and leisure for both the locals and visitors.

Much of the old town has fallen to progress but a walk through the streets will still capture the history and character of Burntisland between the 16th and 20th centuries. The walk starts at the Tourist Office and covers about four kilometres taking approximately two hours.

First of all let us delve into the past and find out why the present town name of Burntisland is steeped in mystery. In the 12th century the area was known as the Parish of Kingorne Wester and due to an abundance of rabbits was also referred to as Coneygarland - coneys being an old name for rabbits. The name Burntisland came from ancient folklore which would have us believe that Fishermen lived in primitive huts on Green Island - now the site of the present shipyard. One day a devastating fire burnt the huts - hence the simple name of Bruntisland or Burntisland superceded Green Island. It is interesting to note that the old Scots word 'brunt' means burnt and 'bruntlin' means a burnt moor. Even so nineteen different spellings have come to light in the Royal Charter and Town Court Books with mentions of Brintiland, Bruntyland, Bertiland, Bruntisland and Birtyland to name but a few.

A Royal Charter was granted by James VI in June, 1541 with the prime purpose of forming a burgh and developing the harbour into a naval port. This charter was never confirmed by Parliament and it was James VI who gave 'our burgh and port (now called Port of Grace)' a new charter in December, 1586.

Original Coat of Arms as displayed over the doorway to the Magistrates Room in the Town Hall.

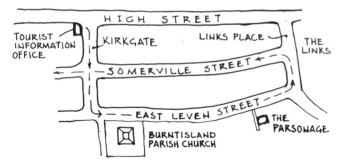

James V, however, was instrumental in the development of Burntisland and the granting of the charter gave the town its first chance of prosperity. New piers were built, shipbuilding flourished and with the harbour used as a naval base Burntisland became the second most important seaport in the Firth of Forth, behind Leith. Consequently the town expanded around the harbour and whereas this area grew in importance the old Kirkton area diminished. The Kirkton was also unable to cope with an increasing population and proposals were put forward for a new Church near the harbour, all as instructed in the charter.

In April 1589 Burntisland's first Provost, John Clapen, called for financial support for a new church at a convention of the Royal Burghs in St. Andrews. The appeal was successful and the building of the new church started in 1592 and was completed by 1595.

The aftermath of the Reformation in 1559 was still very much evident and this may well have influenced the design of the new church. It was reputedly modelled on either the Old North Church in Amsterdam or St. Catherines in Rotterdam and there is no questioning the Dutch influence as demonstrated by the central tower. The choice of the unusual square plan with a central pulpit was to emphasise the equality of all believers.

Today the Parish Church still stands at the top of the Kirkgate as a living memory to the ideals of these Reformers, and perhaps it is this unique design which has ensured that the Church has survived for 400 years.

The interior is indeed special and the two tiers of box pews wrapped around the massive stone pillars create an intimate atmosphere for the central sanctuary and pulpit. Both the pulpit and the Magistrates Pew were built in 1606. Originally the Pew was built for Sir Robert Melville of Rossend Castle and his coat of arms with that of his wife Dame Joanna Hamilton are set in the panelling at the back of the Pew. When the Town Council acquired Rossend Castle the Pew was named the Magistrates Pew and was used at the ceremony of the Kirkin' o' the Council until 1975. Today it is only used by visiting dignitaries. The old Burntisland coat of arms is painted onto the top of the Pew Canopy.

The Parish Church is the only Scots Church where the position of all the Guild Seats is still marked with seats for the schoolmaster, baker, farmer, butcher, maltster and tailor; a sailors loft for the mariners and pews for the laird and gentry. The insignia still exist in their original position along the fronts of the galleries which were built between 1602 to 1630. The panels were all restored between 1907 and 1910 by local painter and historian Andrew Young.

The Magistrates' Pew

Bakers' or Baxters' Panel

J79L9H42

Mastermariner of 17th century

The Guilds had the right to control trade within the Burgh on condition that they looked after their poorer members. During the Feasts of St. Peter and St. John which lasted a week the Guilds allowed non-members to sell manufactured goods to the local townsfolk on payment of a fee. These fees were originally imposed by the Church for people contravening the religious nature of the Feasts by trading and were continued by the Guilds. Non members of the Guilds were also allowed to sell perishable goods such as bread, dairy produce and meat three days a week under certain conditions. Firstly they had to pay a fee for this privilege and secondly they could only sell their products at the Cross at a price fixed by the Burgh.

The Parish Church stands as a landmark for the ships sailing in the Firth of Forth and not surprisingly many of the Guild signs represent the strong links that Burntisland has with the sea. Hanging from one of the pillars is a model of the warship, the Great Michael which was built at Burntisland in the 16th century.

Over the main doorway to the Church is an inverted anchor suggesting that the sailors and fishermen had a strong faith in God to help protect them from the mercy of the seas. An external stair on the east side of the Church allowed the seamen to leave the Sailors' Loft at their convenience incase a sermon clashed with the departure of their ship.

In 1601 James VI stayed at Rossend Castle en route to the General Assembly at St. Andrews. Unfortunately he injured his shoulder while out riding and consequently instructed the General Assembly to meet instead at Burntisland Parish Church on 12th May. During the Assembly proposals were put forward for a new translation of the Bible to eradicate any errors. This was heartily approved by both James VI and the Assembly. The Union of the Crowns in 1603 resulted in James VI ruling from London and therefore the revision of the Bible was completed in England. This Authorised Version was then printed in 1611 and used throughout the world for more than 350 years until it was succeeded by a new translation in 1970.

The Church and controversy were never far apart and in 1638 the Rev. John Michaelson was at odds with the wishes of the congregation when he refused to read the National Covenant from the pulpit. Eventually after strict instructions from the Burgh officials he grudgingly bowed to their wishes and also allowed the Covenant to be signed in the Church.

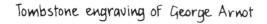

Tombstone engraving of George Arnot

Burntisland Parish Church

In the Church lobby there are several interesting items including a 13th century wooden collecting dish, a 16th century bronze alms dish from the old Kirkton church, a Baskerville Bible dated 1792 and an extract from the minutes of the Convention of Royal Burghs held on 12th April, 1589 recording Provost Clapens request for funds to build a new church.

Out in the Churchyard the largest memorial, dated 1689 stands on the east side of the Church. The initials AW/IB and JW/EO represent Andrew Watson and his wife Isobelle Boswell and John Watson and his wife Euphamie Orrock. It was John Watson who established 'Watson's Mortification'. This originally allowed for three widowed women by the names of Watson, Boswell and Orrock the benefits of a rent free house in the area known as Somerville Square. This continued until 1898 when the house fell into disrepair and in 1956 the property was bought by Burntisland Town Council for redevelopment. Today Watson's Mortification is run by Kirkcaldy District Council, who in keeping with the tradition pay the house rent of three widows in the town. In the shadow of the Binn Leith Avenue, Livingston Drive and MacRae Crescent are collectively known as Widows Land. Another gravestone depicts George Arnot - a local worthy who was renowned for his remarkable memory and storytelling. He would listen to a sermon then repeat it word for word to anyone unable to attend. He died in 1850 in tragic circumstances and local people donated money for his gravestone, which has a carving of George and his familiar wheelbarrow.

In 1843 the country was in upheaval over the question of whether Royalty or Kirk members should appoint ministers to the Church. In what was labelled the Great Disruption the Rev. Dr. Cooper led nearly all the congregation from the Parish Church to form a branch of the Free Church of Scotland. Ironically this new church was located adjacent to the old Parish Church. As if to rub salt in the wounds the resonant toll of the new church bell exposed the old bell as being cracked. A new bell was soon installed but over zealous celebrations by the workmen accidently cracked the new bell.

As previously mentioned the Parish Church replaced an older church at Kirkton. Only the ruins now remain as a reminder of the early days of Christianity when David I granted that land to Dunfermline Abbey in 1130. The Church was consecrated by David de Bernham, the Bishop of St. Andrews in 1243 and served as the main place of worship in the area until the 16th century. Two special ceremonies have taken place at the ruined church this century. On the 8th June, 1930 a service was held at the old church to celebrate 800 years since David I granted the land. Then on the 10th September 1967 a special thanksgiving service was held in the churchyard to commemorate 400 years of Reformed worship.

Further down East Leven Street is the Parsonage – a tribute to George Hay Forbes who was born in Edinburgh in 1821. In spite of being crippled from an early age he was a remarkable man. He studied logic, mathematics, Greek, Latin and French, travelled extensively through Europe and was widely respected for his views on religion. In 1848 he was ordained in Burntisland and the following year he started a school in premises now occupied by the Inchview Hotel in Kinghorn Road. Not satisfied with this arrangement he built his own school and residence now known as the Parsonage.

Forbes had an amazing talent and could converse in about twenty languages with an overall knowledge of about fifty languages. Therefore he set himself the task of publishing the Book of Ecclesiastes in various languages including Hebrew, Greek, Arabic and Latin to name a few. In order to carry out the work Forbes formed the Pitsligo Press in Burntisland and tediously set the type himself for all his translations. His energies were also channelled into being Provost of Burntisland in 1869 but he then resigned over a dispute connected with the building of the new dock.

When Forbes died in 1875 the Parsonage and School were complete and construction had started on a church nearby. This was later abandoned and bought over by the North British Railway Company who converted the building into flats. It was later acquired as a drill hall for the local Territorial Forces and is presently owned by Burntisland District Pipe Band.

The Parsonage

Pediment in Somerville Street

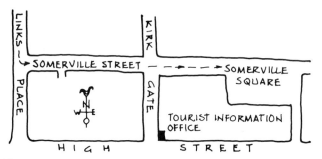

From Links Place we turn left into Somerville Street which leads to Somerville Square. In years gone by this area has been known as Midgait or Back Street or Quality Street - the latter referring to the medieval days when the rich merchants lived here. By the mid-20th century Quality Street was a slum and plans were drawn up to improve the area.

The group of 16th and 17th century buildings on the south side were retained and the street was widened to accommodate the motor car and allow in extra daylight. A square was then created to link up with pedestrian ways between the Railway Station and the High Street, and the existing Blacks Close was resited to pass under an open access bridge. The original close entrance is now the vehicle entrance to the Police Station and is marked by a stone, dated 1736, which is built into the nearby wall.

During alterations to no. 28 painted ceiling boards were uncovered in a room on the second floor. They were carefully removed and are now stored at the Ministry of Works at Edinburgh Castle. The new redevelopment scheme with its flats, maisonettes and terraced houses was designed by architects Wheeler and Sprossan and won a Saltire Society Housing Award. A terraced housing development along the south side of Somerville Street won a Civic Trust Award for Burntisland Town Council.

A plaque at no 28 informs us that this was the house of Vice Admiral Sir William Fairfax and his daughter Mary Somerville. Sir William (1738-1813) joined the British Navy in 1750 and had a distinguished naval career. In 1759 he was present at Quebec when the city was captured by General Wolfe but later suffered four years imprisonment when captured by the French in 1778. At the Battle of Camperdown in 1796 Fairfax was Flag Captain to Admiral Duncan when the British trounced the Dutch Fleet. Fairfax was highly commended for his part in the battle and was knighted for his efforts. He commanded HMS Venerable until 1801 and was then appointed Vice Admiral in 1806.

His daughter Mary Somerville (1780 -1872) was born at a time when the education of women was frowned upon. Undeterred Mary taught herself mathematics, mechanics and astronomy and in 1831 published her first book 'The Mechanism of the Heavens'. It was well received and all the 750 copies were sold at Cambridge University. In recognition of her endeavours she was elected an Honorary Member of the Royal Astronomical Society. This was the first of many honorary posts awarded to this remarkable woman. Her fame and talents were noticed by the Prime Minister, Sir Robert Peel and he recommended that the King grant her a pension of £300 per annum. Mary wrote other books including 'Physical Geography' and 'Molecular and Microscopic Science' which were all published in various languages. Both Somerville College at Oxford and Somerville House at Brisbane High School for girls in Australia are named after one of the greatest Scotswoman of all times.

Somerville Square

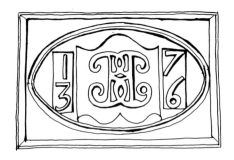  

At no. 25 a double marriage lintel is built into the wall with the date 1688. It refers to the very same people whose names were inscribed on the large memorial in the Parish Churchyard. The house at no. 28 was first owned by Captain Watson in 1596 and passed through the hands of many famous people including John Watson, The Orrocks of that Ilk, Alexander Leslie (later Lord Lindores) and shipmaster William Grieg until it was bought by Vice-Admiral Fairfax in 1789.

Next door to no. 28 is the Masonic Lodge and its most famous resident was General James Robertson born at nearby Newbigging in 1720. Robertson sailed to North America in 1756 and was appointed Major General of the Royal Troops raised in America. In 1779 he became the Civil Governor of New York and later died in London in 1788. Further along, the two houses with external stairs are known as Watson's West Tenement, which contained the four houses left to the schoolmaster and three widows as mentioned in Watson's Mortification.

We now leave Somerville Square by the modern pend which leads us into the High Street. On our right are two marriage lintels from the existing building which stood on this site and was demolished in 1957. The initials RR and AM refer to Richard Ross and Ann Michaelson, daughter of the Rev. John Michaelson who was minister of the Parish Church in the 1630's. On our left in the High Street are the white crowstepped gables of the Star Tavern which was built in 1671 and has been a tavern since 1898.

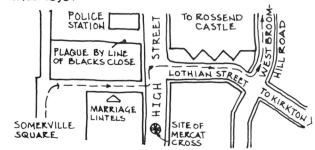

We now head up Lothian Street past yet another 1960's housing scheme which won a Saltire Society Housing Award. Turn left into West Broomhill Road and further on the approach to the Castle is marked by a large stone archway which displays three coats of arms dated 1119, 1382 and 1563. The Castle was built in 1119 and known as Burntisland Castle until 1777 when the new owner, Murdoch Campbell from Skye decided on the change of name to Rossend - Ross being Gaelic for a promontory.

Initially the Castle was the medieval residence of the Duries who were Abbots of Dunfermline. In the tumult following the Reformation Abbot George Durie was responsible for the safety of a richly decorated silver cask which contained the sacred remains of St. Margaret, Queen to Malcolm Canmore in the 11th century. The cask was concealed in the Castle for many years before being smuggled overseas to Antwerp where it mysteriously disappeared. During times of war the Castle was a key stronghold with a commanding position overlooking the Firth of Forth. The French General D'Oysel was based here in 1560 when his troops captured the Castle. By coincidence his main adversary, Sir William Kirkcaldy of Grange, was given the Castle as a reward for his services during the Reformation. Even though Kirkcaldy fought against Mary Queen of Scots at Langside he stoutly held Edinburgh Castle for her for three long years. On surrendering in 1573 he was promptly executed and Burntisland Castle was passed on to his son-in-law Sir Robert Melville.

Gateway to the Castle

Rossend Castle

Mary Queen of Scots stayed at the Castle on her journey through Fife in 1563. Her overnight stop is remembered for the unwanted but amorous advances of a French poet Chastellard who was discovered hiding in her bedroom. This was especially foolish as he had just been pardoned for entering the Queens bedchamber at Holyrood Palace. This second offence could not be overlooked and Chastellard was swiftly executed at the Mercat Cross in St. Andrews.

The Castle had many owners down through the centuries but gradually fell into ruin through lack of attention and was due for demolition in 1962. Strong opposition, two public enquiries and 13 years later the Castle was sold by Burntisland Town Council to architects Robert Hurd & Partners and L.A. Rolland & Partners. With the help of grants from the Historic Council Buildings for Scotland they restored the Castle to its present state. For their careful restoration of the Castle the Firm was awarded the 'R.I.C.S. and The Times Conservation Award'.

In 1957 when the Castle was a crumbling ruin vandals unwittingly revealed an ancient open beam ceiling which was originally part of the ground floor armoury and covered an area of approximately $9 \times 6 m^2$. The ceiling consisted of many individual paintings depicting birds, animals, hunting scenes, the Crusades and emblems including the Coat of Arms of Sir Robert Melville, an owner of the Castle. This confirmed that the ceiling was painted between 1594 and 1621. In order to save the ceiling from further damage Burntisland Town Council donated it to the National Museum of Antiquities in Edinburgh.

Painted ceiling at Rossend Castle

Near the Castle is the site of the old Sea Mill. In olden times this was cleverly operated as the incoming tide was trapped behind the Mill Dam. The water covered an area of nearly 12 acres and with the use of sluices the outgoing water could keep the Mill in operation for nearly 14 hours a day. The granting of the Charter to Burntisland created a dispute with the Castle that raged for years. The Castle owners stubbornly maintained that the townsfolk were legally bound to grind their meal at the Sea Mill and nowhere else. This monopoly angered the Town Council and eventually they built their own Mill in 1711.

The implications of Burntisland being developed as a naval base in 1541 meant that it became embroiled in war. As early as 1542 war broke out between Scotland and England and it was not till the treaty of Boulogne between France and England in 1550 that relative peace settled over Scotland.

In December 1559 the Protestant Lords of the Congregation opposed the Queen Regent - Mary of Guise from France. In order to combat this threat it was in the interests of the Queen Regent to control both the ports of Leith and Burntisland. This would also give her a base for controlling Fife and organising an attack on the Protestant stronghold of St Andrews. Consequently 2500 French troops led by General D'Oysel set off from Leith via the ford at Stirling to attack Burntisland from the west. Simultaneously reinforcements set sail from Leith to ensnare Burntisland in a pincer movement. The French troops met little resistance and easily captured Burntisland. During the occupation of the town the experienced war veteran, Kirkcaldy of Grange, with 600 mounted troops continually harassed the French at every opportunity.

On 24th January, 1560 eight large English warships dropped anchor in the Firth of Forth effectively blockading the French ships and garrison in Burntisland. They also captured the French munition and store ships forcing the French troops to withdraw from Burntisland and return to Leith.

In 1588 the threat of the Spanish Armada spurred Scotland into preparing for war and Burntisland was one of the many muster areas where troops were ordered to assemble for military training. In 1627 new fortifications were built around the town and harbour as Charles I had openly supported the Huguenots of La Rochelle which sparked off fears of invasion.

Following the execution of Charles I the Scots Covenanters still stubbornly supported the monarchy by accepting Charles II as King. This forced Oliver Cromwell's hand and he invaded Scotland with an army of 16,000 men on 22nd July, 1650. After a decisive victory at Dunbar Cromwell set up camp in Edinburgh and made plans to invade Fife in September with Burntisland and Kinghorn earmarked for the first assault. The Scots Parliament had not been idle, however, and since June they had intensified military preparations including the fortification of Burntisland. Major General Leslie was appointed Military Commander and extra troops were drafted in from Dundee to increase the number of men at his command to 500. The town's sea defences against naval attack were also reinforced and to counter any landward attack gun batteries were mounted on the East and West Broomhills.

The English had total command of the Firth of Forth and on 29th January, 1651 General Monk with 1500 troops and supporting warships tried to invade Fife. The English warships and shore batteries briefly exchanged fire with little damage but then a combination of bad seamanship and a sudden strong gale force wind caused the attack to flounder and the English fleet limped back to Leith. Two further attacks were carried out in the spring but these half hearted attempts seemed to be mere feints in order to contain as many Scots troops as possible in Fife. In mid-July, however, Colonel Overton succeeded in landing at North Queensferry in the face of fierce Scots resistance but reinforcements, led by General Lambert, cornered the Scots army at Pitreavie and mercilessly slaughtered over 5000 men.

Faced by an attack from the west and bombardment from the English warships Burntisland Town Council started negotiations for surrender to prevent the pillage and slaughter which would surely follow defeat. A stray cannon ball reputedly landed in the Provost's China shop and this hastened negotiations. The outcome greatly favoured the town and the garrison was allowed to disperse unharmed - perhaps in an attempt to persuade other towns to surrender. Having secured victory Cromwell then arrived by ferry from Leith and probably stayed in either the Castle or at no. 35 High Street. He was suitably impressed with the harbour facilities and remarked on this in a letter confirming a successful invasion of Fife. In August Cromwell withdrew his army to Leith but an English garrison was to remain in Burntisland for a further nine years until 1660. It was a heavy financial burden for the town to carry and it wallowed under the strain long after the garrison left until the town was declared bankrupt in 1692.

A return to more peaceful times gave Burntisland the chance to recapture lost trade but by 1665 Charles II was waging war on Holland. In 1666 the Privy Council issued Letters of Marque to selected shipmasters which gave them a licence to act as privateers for a share of the spoils of war. During 1666 and 1667 many captured Dutch vessels with their cargo were brought back to Leith, Kirkcaldy and Methil; but the Burntisland shipmasters seemed to revel in their role as privateers and were singled out by the Dutch for retaliatory action.

Consequently in April 1667 a fleet of 30 Dutch ships stormed into the Firth of Forth. Initially the Dutch were mistaken for a friendly English fleet and almost caught the shore defences napping. Even though ships lay trapped in Burntisland harbour the privateers managed to land 50 cannon to reinforce the shore batteries. During a three hour exchange of gunfire the Dutch fleet bombarded Burntisland with nearly 500 shots. When additional Dutch ships arrived to strengthen the attack a treacherous west wind once again came to the rescue of the defenders and made sailing conditions impossible, thus forcing the Dutch fleet to retreat. Surprisingly very little damage was reported but perhaps this was an early example of press censorship.

Rossend Castle

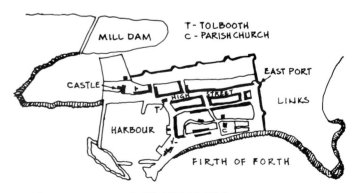

MAP OF BURNTISLAND ABOUT 1745

1-3 Harbour Place

The above 17th century building stands on the site of the old Tolbooth which was built in 1616 and demolished in 1843.

In these troubled times Burntisland often played a key role in the military campaigns that were necessary to keep law and order. For instance in 1689 Viscount Dundee raised the standard for James II in the far north and Government troops were shipped over to Burntisland to prepare for their march north to the Highlands. Later, during the 1715 Jacobite Rebellion the Government ordered all Burntisland ferries to restrict their crossings to Leith and considered disabling all fishing boats along the Fife coast to prevent a Jacobite crossing to the Lothians. One night a Government ship with a cargo of supposedly 3000 muskets docked at Burntisland harbour en route to the north. This snippet of news was passed to John Sinclair, son of the 8th Lord Sinclair of Dysart, who immediately rode to Perth to consult with the Earl of Mar. After much discussion Sinclair was given command of a force of 160 men and ordered to capture the ship. Even though he succeeded a mere 300 muskets were found on board and this involvement in the Rebellion cost him the succession to his father's title.

Later, Mackintosh of Borlum captured Rossend Castle for the Jacobites. Although initial plans to ferry troops over to Leith were thwarted by a strong navy presence in the Forth the Jacobites continued to bring boats into the Burntisland harbour in readiness for a crossing. This was all part of a clever ruse and while warships bombarded the Castle, Mackintosh marched most of his troops at night to the east neuk fishing villages and from there crossed over to the Lothians. Shortly afterwards Government troops regained control of the Castle.

Railway Station

We now retrace our steps from the Castle and cut down Castle Street to the junction of the High Street and Harbour Place where the corner building is the last survivor of a row of 17th century buildings. Up till the 18th century the harbour was located on the far side of the railway built in 1890 to link up with the Forth Rail Bridge.

In the 1840's the Edinburgh and Northern Railway Company proposed to build a line north from the harbour over the Town Links. Amid much controversy the Town Council agreed to the sale and the benefits of this rail link were immediate. Trade increased and Burntisland was more accessible as the town developed into a tourist resort. The railway station was built in 1847 alongside the old manse, built in 1823, and converted into the Forth Hotel for the ferry. In 1844 the Prince Albert Pier was built so that a regular passenger service could operate between Burntisland and Granton. This was organised by the Duke of Buccleugh and Sir John Gladstone, father of Prime Minister William Gladstone. Later, in March 1850 the first rail-ferry in the world operated between the two ports. The passenger ferry continued until 1952 but was revived in 1991 with regular crossings over the Forth in the summer months. When the Forth Rail Bridge opened in 1890 Burntisland was greatly affected as it lost the benefits of being a terminus and was relegated to just another railway station on the route round the Fife coast. In 1914 an appalling rail disaster occurred when the London to Aberdeen express train collided with a goods train. The express train was derailed and ploughed through a wall onto the Links. Both the driver and fireman were killed and twelve people were seriously injured.

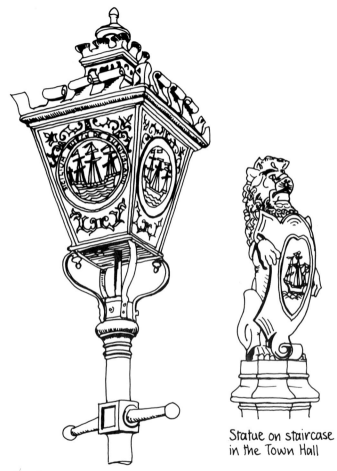

The Burntisland Provost's Lamp - now at Kirkcaldy District Council Offices

Statue on staircase in the Town Hall

We continue on up the High Street passing the Public Library, built in 1906 and gifted to the people of Burntisland by Andrew Carnegie - the Dunfermline born Scot who made his millions in the steel industry in the U.S.A. Above the library is an Edwardian Fair Exhibition and a display depicting the story of Burntisland. The Town Hall stands alongside the Library and was built in 1843 to replace the old Tolbooth which had stood since 1616 down by the harbour. A west wing was added in 1903 and renovations were carried out to the Council Chambers in the 1950's. Burntisland Town Council appointed its first Provost John Clapen or Clephane on 21st October, 1586 after being granted a Charter in 1541. At the time Burntisland was listed as the 17th Burgh at the Convention of Royal Burghs. Indeed the Provost's Chain of Office was one of the oldest in all Scotland and was presented in 1818 by the Fishcurers Society of Burntisland. The seal on the reverse side of the Chain represents a fish and the legendary success of the herring industry.

At the foot of the stairs to the Council Chamber stands a large bell bought by the Town Council from Berwick-on-Tweed in 1619. It was used in the Tolbooth until it cracked in 1679 and had to be sent to Holland for recasting. Other items worthy of note are the original Coat of Arms depicted over the doorway to the Magistrates Room; the Royal Arms of Scotland, dated 1382 and originally hung on the vestibule hall at Rossend Castle; the Royal Arms of Scotland as most likely used in the reign of Charles I nearly 350 years ago. Quite appropriately for Burntisland a fully rigged ship hangs in the Council Chamber emphasising the Town's strong link with the sea.

Among the many pictures hanging on the Council Chamber walls are a copy of the original Charter of 1541, a Certificate of Registration of the Coat of Arms of the Burgh dated 6th April, 1938 and a list of the Provosts of the Burgh since 1586.

The highest honour Burntisland Town Council could award to any person was to make them a Freeman of the Burgh. This rare honour was bestowed on Sir John Gladstone in 1840 for starting a ferry service in Burntisland; on millionaire Andrew Carnegie in 1907 for donating funds for the building of a local library and on Miss Daisy MacRae in 1966 who was Burntisland's first woman councillor, first woman magistrate, first woman Justice of the Peace and the first woman Burgess.

In February 1975 Burntisland Town Council bestowed this unique honour of Freedom of the Burgh on three men who had given a lifetime's service to the Town. They were 'Bailie' R.M. Livingstone, an active member of the Council for many years including a stint as Provost between 1953 to 1958. In 1953 he was awarded the Coronation Medal and was also a noted local historian who documented the town in great detail; Rev. Colin McDonald who was the minister of Erskine United Free Church for 37 years and who had the distinction of twice being Moderator of his Church's General Assembly and Dr. Robert Smith, who practised in the town for more than 40 years and took a keen interest in local affairs. In May 1975 Burntisland Town Council was replaced by Kirkcaldy District Council as part of local government reorganisation. It was the end of an era spanning nearly 400 years.

Town Hall

The Union of Parliaments in 1707 and the crushing of the Jacobite Rebellion at Culloden Moor in 1746 contributed in various ways to the continued demise of Burntisland in the 18th century.

In 1786, however, an enterprising William Young established a distillery at the Grange. It occupied a six acre site and with a plentiful water supply from the nearby Dunearn Loch 200,000 gallons of Old Burntisland lowland malt were produced every year. The Company provided its own coopers, joiners, excisemen, stables, fire engine and gas works and was a thriving business. In 1914 Youngs became part of the Scottish Malt Distilleries and although the buildings stand empty today the site offers great potential for housing development.

The turning point in Burntisland's fortunes was the unexplained reappearance of vast shoals of herring in Scottish waters between 1793 and 1803. At its peak nearly 500 fishing boats would be crammed into the harbour unloading their catch for the eight herring curing factories on shore. The herring boon provided work for many associated trades including boatbuilders, coopers, porters, hirers and merchants and thus brought considerable wealth to Burntisland. During this time trade naturally increased and imports of tar, pitch, wine and timber were countered by exports of herring, whitefish, salmon, salt, hides and coal. Indeed it was the coal industry and the arrival of the railway to Burntisland that ensured continued prosperity.

A new dock was built in 1876 to cope with the vast volumes of coal being exported from Fife. Unfortunately for Burntisland a dock was built at Methil in 1888 which quickly established itself as a serious competitor because of its close location to the East Fife coalfields. To counter this a new dock was opened at Burntisland in 1901 but in spite of this successful venture coal exports had dwindled to rock bottom shortly after 1945.

In 1913 Burntisland offered an ideal location for the British Aluminium Company with good port facilities, good rail connections and plentiful coal and water supplies. As a result land was purchased at Kirkton and by 1917 the plant was converting the imported bauxite into alumina. Originally the alumina was sent to the smelters at Fort William and Kinlochleven for convertion into metal. In 1982 British Aluminium merged with the Canadian firm Alcan and a new plant was opened in 1984 to produce superfines. These are used in various products from toothpaste and pottery to fire retardants.

The Burntisland Shipbuilding Company was founded by the Ayre Brothers in 1918 and built ships for firms throughout the world. With a long tradition of boatbuilding Burntisland soon earned worldwide recognition and 'Burntisland Built' became synonymous with sound design, construction and economy. The first vessel S.S. Sunbank was launched in 1919 and during the 1930's the Company built Economy Cargo Ships to help counteract the Depression. During the Second World War the aircraft carrier Empire MacKendrick was built in the Yards.

The aircraft carrier had a dual purpose of shipping food supplies from Canada and the U.S.A. as well as providing fighter escorts for the Atlantic convoys. The Yard went into liquidation, as far as shipbuilding was concerned, in 1968 but other associated industries have developed with the recent construction of oil rig platforms. On the sporting front the Yard ran a football team which started up in the 1920's. In 1938 the Shipyard XI met Celtic in the Scottish Cup. With the score level at 3-3 and twenty minutes to go Celtic were awarded a penalty. They duly scored and went on to win 8-3.

Another industry which briefly established itself in Burntisland was a Vitriol works. It was based at the Lammerlaws and started up in the late 18th century to produce sulphuric acid for bleaching and tanning. By 1831 it had closed down. In 1936 an open air swimming pool was built in the Lammerlaws and provided invigorating enjoyment for those hardy swimmers who braved the icy waters. By the late 1970's the pool was in a dilapidated condition and was demolished. The pool was such a boon to the town that plans are afoot to build a new sports and swimming pool complex to cater for both the visitors and local townsfolk.

The Burntisland Traders Association are a group of local businesses who are involved in promoting Burntisland. They are presently involved with Fife Enterprise, Fife Region and Kirkcaldy District Council on a scheme which will upgrade the shopfronts to the High Street.

'The Burntisland Traders Association welcomes you to our picturesque town and we hope that you will enjoy your visit. Whether you are looking for a Bar Lunch or something more substantial, a new dress or a newsagent, be sure to call in at any one of our members businesses - you will see the Burntisland Traders Association Symbol prominently displayed in their window. We're here to serve, and please remember to tell your friends to visit us - we'll give them a warm welcome too.'

We now walk on to the end of the High Street where the impressive Old Port Buildings, built in 1899 stand near the site of the old East Port. From 1635 the main entrance into the town was through the East Port which was later demolished in 1843. It was here that part of Hackston of Rathillet's body was displayed as a warning to the Covenanters after Hackston's role in the cruel murder of Archbishop Sharp on Magus Muir in 1679. Two pillars from from the old Port now stand at the entrance to the Links which was granted in the Charter to the townsfolk. The Links served three purposes. They provided the opportunity for the drying of fishing nets and clothes, the grazing of livestock and a facility for recreation.

This included golf which was played on the Links as early as 1668. The Burntisland Golf House Club, founded in 1797 is the 11th oldest club in Scotland and the 3rd oldest in Fife behind the Royal and Ancient Golf Club and Crail Golfing Society. The first course of 15 holes was laid out over the Links but general congestion plus the intrusion of the Railway reduced the course to 5 holes. Consequently the Club took on a lease of 12 acres on the High Bents between Burntisland and Kinghorn. By 1894 further expansion was required due to the popularity of the game and a new course was opened over Dodhead Farm in 1897. Soon after James Braid and Harry Vardon, who had won 11 British Open Championships between them, played over the course on 15th July 1901 but no scorecards exist to confirm the result.

Across from the Golf Club House is a path that leads up through the trees to the top of the Binn. The walk is well worth the panoramic view and an indicator at the summit pinpoints towns and distant hills in the surrounding countryside. In the 19th century the nearby Binn village housed those people involved with the Binnend Oil Company. The decline of the oil and shale industry, however, quickly snuffed out this small community and the village is now a fragmented ruin.

From the East Port we continue our walk along Kinghorn Road. A strict policy of prohibiting any development on the Links has allowed those buildings on Kinghorn Road a magnificent view out over the Links and Firth of Forth to Edinburgh. It is an ideal setting for the Inchview Hotel which occupies part of the Georgian Terrace along the Kinghorn Road. The Inchview Hotel caters for all visitors whether involved in leisure, business or pleasure and the facilities and Inchview Restaurant are commended by the Scottish Tourist Board.

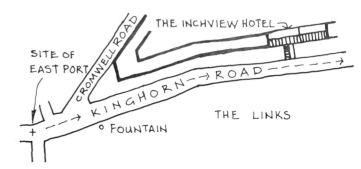

Erskine United Free Church

The Fairs on the Links were initially markets for the sale of produce or hiring fairs where agricultural labourers were hired for a year. Today the summer fair is mainly for entertainment and along with the Highland Games are an established and important part of Burntisland's festivities. The Highland Games are held every third Monday in July and date back to 1654. Other summer attractions on the Links are paddling pools, putting greens, swings and trampolenes to complement a safe sandy beach.

At the eastern end of the Links stands the Erskine United Free Church built in 1903. The five light stained glass window was designed on the theme 'The Light of The World' and dates from 1921. Kinghorn Road now includes Craigholm Crescent and Dr. Chalmers who led the great disruption of the Church of Scotland stayed at no. 14. Another famous inhabitant of Burntisland was Alexander Orrock of Silliebawbie who was Mintmaster for Scotland in 1538 and responsible for the introduction of the bawbee - the old Scots halfpenny.

Beyond the outskirts of Burntisland stands the Kingswood Hotel set back in the trees from the Kinghorn Road. It was originally built in 1851 as the home of the Johnson family who were involved in the sugar trade in Jamacia. Recently the hotel was extended to provide a function suite, eight ensuite bedrooms and a large conservatory and is now a Scottish Tourist Board four crown commended hotel.

Kingswood Hotel

Kinghorn Road, Burntisland, Fife. KY3 9LL.
telephone: 0592 872329. Fax: 0592 873123.

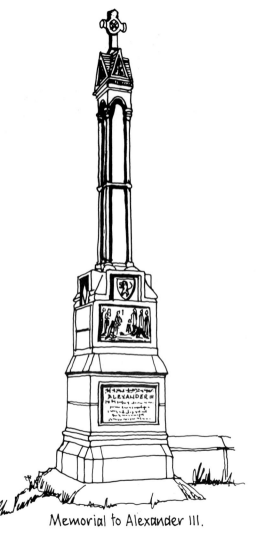

Memorial to Alexander III.

Just past the Kingswood Hotel on the road to Kinghorn is a simple memorial at the foot of the cliffs to Alexander III. In March, 1286 Alexander set off from Edinburgh to be with his newly wed wife who was waiting at Kinghorn Castle. The weather was most foul and the ferrymen at Queensferry reluctantly set sail at the Royal Command. Ignoring further warnings Alexander continued along the coast past Burntisland, and in the total darkness of that stormy night his horse stumbled throwing him to an untimely death. It proved to be a national calamity for Scotland especially as his successor, the young Maid of Norway, died soon after. The throne of Scotland now had no firm contender allowing Edward I of England to arrogantly claim sovereignship over Scotland. This created great enmity between the two countries and resulted in the War of Independence which culminated in a decisive Scots victory at Bannockburn in 1314.

From the memorial we have an excellent view across the bay towards Burntisland. Both Rossend Castle and the Parish Church are easily identifiable due to their commanding positions high above the town. It is very appropriate that they are still standing today as they represent a precious link with the history of Burntisland which dates back nearly nine hundred years.

THE END

ILLUSTRATIONS

Burntisland Coat of Arms	4
Original Coat of Arms	6
Magistrates Pew	7
Guild Panels	8
Parish Church	9
The Parsonage	11
Pediment - Somerville Street	12
Somerville Square	13
Plaques & marriage lintels	14
Gateway to Rossend Castle	15
Rossend Castle	16
Painted ceiling	17
Rossend Castle	19
1-3 Harbour Place	20
Railway Station	21
Provost's Lamp	22
Town Hall	23
Burntisland Traders Association	25
The Inchview Hotel	27
Erskine Church	28
Kingswood Hotel	29
Alexander III memorial	30

MAPS

Kirkgate - Somerville St.	6
Somerville St. - Somerville Sq	12
Somerville Sq. - West Broomhill Road	14
Map of Burntisland - 1745.	19
Rossend Castle - High Street	21
East Port - The Links	26

BIBLIOGRAPHY

A History of Golf Clubs in Fife
Burntisland - Early History and People - John J. Blyth
Burntisland Parish Church 400th Anniversary Brochure - by Rev. Jim Monaghan.
Discovering Fife - Raymond Lamont Brown
Fife - The Buildings of Scotland - John Gifford.
Glimpses of Modern Burntisland by ex-Bailie Erskine.
History of Burntisland - Andrew Young.
The Fringes of Fife by John Geddie
The Kingdom of Fife by Theo Lang
The Shores of Fife - Blackie & Son Ltd.
Rossend Castle - Hurd/Rolland Partnership (1977)
Extract from Fife Advertiser 29th April, 1873
Press cuttings on Burntisland - Fife Free Press.

Model of 'The Great Michael' - Burntisland Parish Church

ACKNOWLEDGEMENTS

I am grateful to many local people for their help in providing old books, pamphlets and photographs and in particular their time during the research for this book. Many thanks to :-
Staff at the Tourist Information Office,
Staff at Burntisland Public Library,
Tom Courts, Norman Mackie,
Colin McLaren, Jim Murphy,
Bobby Robertson, Bill & Fiona Rollo,
Brian and Maureen Robson
and a special thanks to
Walter and Lilian Anderson and to my parents, Tom and Betty Pearson.

I am also grateful for the assistance given by local businesses:
Burntisland Traders Association;
Mr & Mrs Peter Black at
The Inchview Hotel;
Mr & Mrs Rankin Bell at the
Kingswood Hotel.

Finally I acknowledge that the location map is based on the Ordnance Survey Map with the permission of the controller of Her Majesty's Stationery Office © Crown Copyright.

J.M.P.

The Author

John M. Pearson was born at St. Andrews, Fife in 1952. He is an architect by profession having graduated with a Bachelor of Architecture degree at Heriot-Watt University, Edinburgh in 1976. Travelled overseas between 1977-1983 and worked in New Zealand and Australia before returning to Scotland. From 1983-1987 he worked for the Edinburgh architects' firm Dick Peddie & McKay at their Invergordon office. Has since completed a four year stint in the London area and is presently based in Teddington, Middlesex. His other publications include :-

A Guided Walk round Inverness

A Guided Walk round St. Andrews

A Guided Walk round Edinburgh

Around North East Fife

St. Andrews - Street Map and Places of Interest.

Edinburgh - The Royal Mile Guide
(text by Colin M. Pearson).

Above publications available from :-
John M. Pearson, 'Lingmoor,'
Carberry Park, Leven, Fife. KY8 4JG
Books £3.50 (inc. P+P)